Jill Prestup

The Book of American
Trade Marks/9
The Annual of Trade Mark Design

David E. Carter

**Book Design
Stephanie Fulton**

First Printing, 1984

ART DIRECTION BOOK COMPANY
10 East 39th Street
New York, NY 10016

(212) 889-6500

Library of Congress Catalog Card Number: 72-76493
International Standard Book Number: 0-88108-020-9
ISBN for Standing Orders for this series: 0910158-38-X

How to submit marks for future volumes.

This book is part of a series which shows good examples of contemporary design of trade marks, corporate symbols and logos.

Designers are invited to submit marks for possible inclusion in future volumes. Work submitted must adhere to the following guidelines:

(1) marks must be sent in the actual size they are to be reproduced in the book. Any marks not meeting this standard will be eliminated from consideration.

(2) do not mount the work.

(3) include the name of the client, and the one name to appear in the credit line as designer.

(4) send a letter giving permission for the marks to be included in the book.

Due to the large amount of material received each year, it is impossible for us to acknowledge receipt of marks.

All material should be sent to: David E. Carter, Trade Marks, P.O. Box 591, Ashland, Kentucky 41105.

8359

8363

8360

8364

8361

8365

8362

8366

8367

8368

8369

8370

8371

8375

8372

8376

8373

8377

8374

8378

8379

The Diplomat

8380

European American Sales Union

FOR JEWELRY, WATCHES AND PRECIOUS STONES

8381

AQUA-O CORPORATION

8382

BABTON Lighting Center

8381   Aqua-O Corporation
        Designer: Spyros Dellaportas

8382   Babton Lighting
        Designer: Spyros Dellaportas

8371   Glaucoma Foundation
        Designer: Spyros Dellaportas

8372   American Property Assoc.
        Designer: Spyros Dellaportas

8373   Richard Rubbins Photographer
        Designer: Spyros Dellaportas

8374   Real Property Management
        Designer: Spyros Dellaportas

8375   Abraham Shapiro A.I.A.
        Designer: Spyros Dellaportas

8376   Printland
        Designer: Spyros Dellaportas

8377   International Research Services Inc.
        Designer: Spyros Dellaportas

8378   Nichiren Shoshu of America
        Designer: Spyros Dellaportas

8379   The Diplomat Condominiums
        Designer: Spyros Dellaportas

8380   European American Sales Union
        Designer: Spyros Dellaportas

8383

8387

8384

8388

8385

8389

8386

8390

8391

8392

8393

8394

8383 Santa Monica Cultural Arts
      Committee
      Designer: Spyros Dellaportas

8384 Napoc. Inc.
      Designer: Spyros Dellaportas

8385 Copan, Inc.
      Designer: Spyros Dellaportas

8386 Ben Bronson
      Designer: Spyros Dellaportas

8387 Panco, Inc.
      Designer: Spyros Dellaportas

8388 George Polycrated & Assoc.
      Designer: Spyros Dellaportas

8389 Napoc, Inc.
      Designer: Spyros Dellaportas

8390 E.A.S.T.
      Designer: Spyros Dellaportas

8391 Spyros Dellaportas
      Designer: Spyros Dellaportas

8392 Barton National
      Designer: Spyros Dellaportas

8393 Copan, Inc.
      Designer: Spyros Dellaportas

8394 Meridian Corporation
      Designer: Spyros Dellaportas

8395

8399

8396

8400

8397

8401

8398

8402

8403

8404

8405

8395 Terra Resources
Designer: Lonnie Whittington

8396 Pat Darum
Designer: Lonnie Whittington

8397 Associated Lithographers
Designer: Lonnie Whittington

8398 Sigma Group
Designer: Lonnie Whittington

8399 Everest '85
Designer: Jean Wong

8400 Applied Micro Solutions
Designer: Al Luna

8401 Mastercraft Plastics
Designer: Al Luna

8402 Mikasa
Designer: Lonnie Whittington
& Al Luna

8403 Arizona Lobster & Seafood Co.
Designer: Jean Wong

8404 Air Scottsdale
Designer: Lonnie Whittington
& Al Luna

8405 Western Education Inc.
Designer: Al Luna

8406 Metalogic
Designer: Lonnie Whittington
& Al Luna

8406

METALOGIC

8407

SKYLINE STEEL

8411

THE ALL NEW

9
1 ABC 2 DEF 3
GHI 4 JKL 5 MNO 6
1 PRS 7 TUV 8 WXY 9 8
? OPER 0 !
4

DIRECTORY
OF HUMAN SERVICES

8408

MICRO LEVEL

8412

8409

8413

8410

8414

8415

Cash
Sullivan
&Cross

8416

8417

8418

8419

8423

8420

8424

8421

8425

8422

8426

8427

Mikasa

8428

Brene

8429

8430

8419   Urokeep
        Designer: Lonnie Whittington

8420   Cybernet Plastics
        Designer: Lonnie Whittington

8421   Kaibab Industries
        Designer: Lonnie Whittington

8422   Arizona Chapter of the American
            Red Cross
        Designer: Lonnie Whittington

8423   Cortez Corp
        Designer: Lonnie Whittington

8424   Data Base
        Designer: Lonnie Whittington

8425   Maricopa County Chapter of the
            American Red Cross
        Designer: Lonnie Whittington
            & Tom Chung

8426   Data Systems of Arizona
        Designer: Lonnie Whittington

8427   Mikasa
        Designer: Jean Wong

8428   Brene Office & Home Furnishings
        Designer: Jean Wong

8429   Hang-Ups
        Designer: Jean Wong

8430   WW3/Papagalos Design & Advertising
        Designer: Jean Wong

8431

8435

8432

8436

8433

8437

8434

8438

8439

8440

8441

8442

8431   Rhythm Aerobics Studio
Designer: Jean Wong

8432   Etienne's French Restaurant
Designer: Jean Wong

8433   The Mews on Tenth Place
Designer: Jean Wong

8434   Pictures
Designer: Jean Wong

8435   Greenbrier Shopping Mall
Designer: Emil M. Cohen

8436   Twelve Oaks Shopping Mall
Designer: Emil M. Cohen

8437   NewPark Shopping Mall
Designer: Emil M. Cohen

8438   Centennial Valley Shopping Mall
Designer: Emil M. Cohen

8439   The Hennesey Construction Co.
Designer: Emil M. Cohen

8440   Burnsville Center Shopping Mall
Designer: Emil M. Cohen

8441   Foxboro Shopping Mall
Designer: Emil M. Cohen

8442   Spring Hill Shopping Mall
Designer: Emil M. Cohen

8443

8447

8444

8448

8445

8449

8446

8450

8451

8452

8453

8454

8443	Louis Joliet Shopping Mall Designer: Emil M. Cohen
8444	Deerbrook Shopping Mall Designer: Emil M. Cohen
8445	Willowbrook Shopping Mall Designer: Emil M. Cohen
8446	Meadowbrook Shopping Mall Designer: Emil M. Cohen
8447	Pinebrook Shopping Mall Designer: Emil M. Cohen
8448	Baybrook Shopping Mall Designer: Emil M. Cohen
8449	Westgate Shopping Mall Designer: Emil M. Cohen
8450	Richland Fashion Mall Designer: Emil M. Cohen
8451	The Evanston Symphony Orchestra Designer: Emil M. Cohen
8452	School Spirit Designer: Emil M. Cohen
8453	The Allen Woods Co. Designer: Emil M. Cohen
8454	Keogh Motivation Plans, Inc. Designer: Emil M. Cohen

8455

8459

Northfield
Township
Arts Council

8456

8460

8457

8461

8458

8462

8463

8464

8455	Music for the Children of Israel Designer: Emil M. Cohen
8456	Am Sholom Congregation Designer: Emil M. Cohen
8457	Communications Research, Inc. Designer: Emil M. Cohen
8458	The Ram Engineering Co. Designer: Emil M. Cohen
8459	Northfield Township Arts Council Designer: Emil M. Cohen
8460	LaSalle Planning Co. Designer: Emil M. Cohen
8461	The Rock Island Railroad Designer: Emil M. Cohen
8462	The Colt Construction Co. Designer: Emil M. Cohen
8463	Emil M. Cohen Designer: Emil M. Cohen
8464	Friends of the Wilmette Public Library Designer: Emil M. Cohen
8465	The Chicago Commoisseur Designer: Emil M. Cohen

8465

8466

8470

8467

8471

8468

8472

8469

8473

8474

8475

8476

8466	La Choy Food Products Designer: Dixon & Parcels Assoc.
8467	Scott Paper Company Designer: Dixon & Parcels Assoc.
8468	Beech-Nut Foods Corp. Designer: Dixon & Parcels Assoc.
8469	Harbor Sweets Ltd. Designer: Dixon & Parcels Assoc.
8470	M&M/Mars Snack Master Div. Designer: Dixon & Parcels Assoc.
8471	R.M. Palmer Company Designer: Dixon & Parcels Assoc.
8472	Gougeon Brothers Inc. Designer: Dixon & Parcels Assoc.
8473	M&M/Mars , Inc. Snack Master Div. Designer: Dixon & Parcels Assoc.
8474	Austin Foods Company Designer: Dixon & Parcels Assoc.
8475	National Industries for the Blind Designer: Dixon & Parcels Assoc.
8476	Georgia Southern College Designer: Dixon & Parcels Assoc.

8477

8481

8478

8482

8479

8483

8480

8484

8485

8486

8487

8488

8477	Krispy Kreme Doughnut Corp. Designer: Dixon & Parcels Assoc.
8478	Bernan Foods Inc. Designer: Dixon & Parcels Assoc.
8479	Superior Pet Products Inc. Designer: Dixon & Parcels Assoc.
8480	Del Monte Designer: Dixon & Parcels Assoc.
8481	National Sea Products Designer: Dixon & Parcels Assoc.
8482	Luminall Paints Inc. Designer: Dixon & Parcels Assoc.
8483	M&M/Mars Snack Master Div. Designer: Dixon & Parcels Assoc.
8484	ITT Continental Banking Company Designer: Dixon & Parcels Assoc.
8485	The Pennsylvania State University Designer: Dixon & Parcels Assoc.
8486	Cadillac Pet Foods, Inc. Designer: Dixon & Parcels Assoc.
8487	Maripac International Designer: Dixon & Parcels Assoc.
8488	Young Drug Products Corp. Designer: Dixon & Parcels Assoc.

8489

8493

8490

8494

8491

8492

8495

8496

8497

8498

8489	Wilber Chocolate Co., Inc. Designer: Dixon & Parcels Assoc.
8490	E.B. Evans Inc. Designer: Dixon & Parcels Assoc.
8491	Superior Pet Products Inc. Designer: Dixon & Parcels Assoc.
8492	ITT Continental Banking Company Designer: Dixon & Parcels Assoc.
8493	Pennsylvania Dutch-Megs Inc. Designer: Dixon & Parcels Assoc.
8494	Borden Inc. Designer: Dixon & Parcels Assoc.
8495	Crest Eastern Corp. Designer: Dixon & Parcels Assoc.
8496	Industrial Valley Bank Designer: Dixon & Parcels Assoc.
8497	The Bachman Company Designer: Dixon & Parcels Assoc.
8498	Dari Farms Designer: Dixon & Parcels Assoc.

8499

BANK
OF MID-JERSEY

8502

8503

8500

PFEIFFER

BONOMO

8501

8504

8505

Action Philadelphia

8506

8507

8499	Bank of Mid-Jersey Designer: Dixon & Parcels Assoc.
8500	Pfeiffer's Foods, Inc. Designer: Dixon & Parcels Assoc.
8501	Bonomo Candy Company Designer: Dixon & Parcels Assoc.
8502	4C Foods Corp. Designer: Dixon & Parcels Assoc.
8503	Gold Medal Candy Corp. Designer: Dixon & Parcels Assoc.
8504	Youngs Drug Products Corp. Designer: Dixon & Parcels Assoc.
8505	Action Philadelphia Designer: Dixon & Parcels Assoc.
8506	Franklin Papers Designer: Douglas Wilson
8507	Paradise Found Designer: Douglas Wilson

8508

The Lincoln Theater

8512

ACCOUNTING RESOURCES INTERNATIONAL

8509

the FOLKS at COMPANY

8513

dexter DATA SYSTEMS INC.

8514

8510

Twin Anchors Marina

8515

8511

Rochester Steel

8516

8517

8518

8519

8520

8524

jazz band

8521

8525

Weber
Management
Dynamics

8522

8526

AMERICA'S FINEST!

8523

8527

8528

8529

8530

8531

8520	Gordon Reese Designer: Douglas Wilson
8521	Spencer Group Designer: Douglas Wilson
8522	The Boats Sail Inn Designer: Douglas Wilson
8523	Sun Ray Products, Inc. Designer: Douglas Wilson
8524	Dixie 5 Designer: Douglas Wilson
8525	Weber Management Designer: Douglas Wilson
8526	Th Cleaners Designer: Doug Granger
8527	Southwind Ultralights, Inc. Designer: Doug Granger
8528	Media National Corporation Designer: Doug Granger
8529	Genesis Network Designer: Doug Granger
8530	Genesis Production Corporation Designer: Doug Granger
8531	Genesis Management Corporation Designer: Doug Granger

8532

8536

SHAW
RESOURCES

8533

8537

8534

8538

MIRRIM

8535

8539

8540

8541

8542

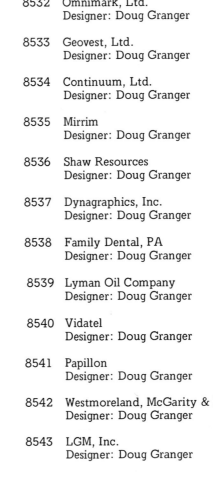

8543

8532	Omnimark, Ltd. Designer: Doug Granger
8533	Geovest, Ltd. Designer: Doug Granger
8534	Continuum, Ltd. Designer: Doug Granger
8535	Mirrim Designer: Doug Granger
8536	Shaw Resources Designer: Doug Granger
8537	Dynagraphics, Inc. Designer: Doug Granger
8538	Family Dental, PA Designer: Doug Granger
8539	Lyman Oil Company Designer: Doug Granger
8540	Vidatel Designer: Doug Granger
8541	Papillon Designer: Doug Granger
8542	Westmoreland, McGarity & Pitts Designer: Doug Granger
8543	LGM, Inc. Designer: Doug Granger

8544

8548

KRISTA'MI

8545

8549

8546

8550

8547

8551

8552

8553

Women in Free Enterprise

8554

8555

FOUR STAR
OIL & GAS CO.

8556

8560

8557

GRANT/
THOMPSON

8561

8558

8562

8559

8563

8564

8565

8566

8567

8556	Christopher National Press Designer: Jim Adams
8557	Grant/Thompson Designer: Jim Adams
8558	T & B Scottdale Contractors Designer: Don Connelly
8559	Electromagnetic Systems Inc. Designer: Don Connelly
8560	Professional Association Management Designer: Don Connelly
8561	Alvin Lee Construction Designer: Don Connelly
8562	Shaw & Parrott Racing Designer: Don Connelly
8563	College Coaches Classic Designer: Don Connelly
8564	Automated Marketing Designer: Don Connelly
8565	Condor Automotive Services Designer: Don Connelly
8566	Newspaper in Education Designer: Don Connelly
8567	The Selin Company Designer: Don Connelly

8568

8572

8569

8573

8574

8570

8571

8575

8576

8577

THE SUN DYNASTY

CHINESE RESTAURANT & LOUNGE

8578

8579

Park Place
S O U T H

8580

8584

8581

8585

8582

8586

8583

8587

8588

8589

8590

8591

8580   HOBIS
       Designer: Don Connelly

8581   Big Heart Award
       Designer: Don Connelly

8582   Cincinnati Zoo
          (proposal)
       Designer: Robert Probst

8583   Cincinnati Zoo
          (proposal)
       Designer: Robert Probst

8584   Cincinnati Zoo
          (proposal)
       Designer: Robert Probst

8585   Cincinnati Zoo
          (proposal)
       Designer: Robert Probst

8586   Cincinnati Zoo
          (proposal)
       Designer: Robert Probst

8587   American General Communications
       Designer: Max A. McDonald

8588   Home Product Installers
       Designer: Max A. McDonald

8589   Max McDonald Design Office
       Designer: Max A. McDonald

8590   Tom Thornburg, Painter
       Designer: Max A. McDonald

8591   Tom's Paint Store
       Designer: Max A. McDonald

8592

8596

8593

8597

8594

8598

8599

8595

8600

Westfield
by-the-railroad

8601

8602

8603

8592 Central Home Health Care
Designer: Max A. McDonald

8593 Sea-Temp Instrument Company
Designer: Max A. McDonald

8594 Formakers
Designer: Max A. McDonald

8595 Marglotex
Designer: Max A. McDonald

8596 Decal Advertising
Designer: Max A. McDonald

8597 Insights West
Designer: Max A. McDonald

8598 KTRE-TV 9
Designer: Debbie Brumfield

8599 Venture Construction Co.
Designer: Debbie Brumfield

8600 Westfield
Designer: Debbie Brumfield

8601 Debbie Brumfield Design
Designer: Debbie Brumfield

8602 Christian Information & Service
      Center
Designer: Debbie Brumfield

8603 Hardwood Designs
Designer: Debbie Brumfield

8604

8608
Frisco

8605
WOMEN'S INTEREST NETWORK

8609
TIMBERLINE HOMES

8606
IMAGES

8610
A LITTLE COUNTRY
Biskits
IN YOUR MOUTH

8607
PALM BEACH CAFE

8611
Heartland
RECORDS

8612

8613

8614

8615

8604 Wenger- Brumfield Advertising
Designer: Debbie Brumfield

8605 Women's Interest Network
Designer: Debbie Brumfield

8606 Images Audio-Visual Services
Designer: The Malone Group

8607 Palm Beach Cafe
Designer: The Malone Group

8608 City Center Discoteque
Designer: The Malone Group

8609 Timberline Homes
Designer: The Malone Group

8610 Restaurant Chain
Designer: The Malone Group

8611 Heartland Record Co.
Designer: The Malone Group

8612 Gourmet Restaurant
Designer: The Malone Group

8613 Ponte Vedra Square
Designer: The Malone Group

8614 Bimini Bay Development
Designer: The Malone Group

8615 Calvary Ministries International
Designer: The Malone Group

8616

8620

8617

8621

8618

8622

8619

8623

8624

8625

8626

8630

SHAPIRO
MELLINGER

8627

8631

8628

8632

8629

8633

G◗◗◗NG PLACES

8634

8635

8636

8637

8638

8641

8639

8642

8640

8643

8644

8645

8646

8638   Ellerman Companies, Inc.
        Designer: Jim Lienhart

8639   Management Organization Inc.
        Designer: Jim Lienhart

8640   General Sintering Corporation
        Designer: Jim Lienhart

8641   Sphere
        Designer: Jim Lienhart

8642   Savings & Loan News
        Designer: Jim Lienhart

8643   Diamond International, Inc.
        Designer: Jim Lienhart

8644   Chicago Graphics, Inc.
        Designer: Jim Lienhart

8645   Tero Corvette
        Designer: Jim Lienhart

8646   Color Communications, Inc.
        Designer: Jim Lienhart

8647

8650

8648

8651

8649

8652

8653

8654

8655

8659

8656

ultimo

8657

8660

PMA

8858

8661

8662

8663

8664

8665

8656 Ultimo
      Designer: Jim Lienhart

8657 Interchange Marketing Corporation
      Designer: Jim Lienhart

8658 Liquidity Fund for Thrifts, Inc.
      Designer: Jim Lienhart

8659 Conrad Bailey Photography
      Designer: Jim Lienhart

8660 W. Clement Stone/
          PMA Communications, Inc.
      Designer: Jim Leinhart

8661 Peter Sagara Photography
      Designer: Jim Lienhart

8662 Dan Morrill
      Designer: Jim Lienhart

8663 Acme Wiley, Inc.
      Designer: Jim Lienhart

8664 Whittle Radon Motley & Hanks
      Designer: Jim Lienhart

8665 Becky Bisioulis
      Designer: Jim Lienhart

8666

8669

8667

8670

Blomstrand Communications Inc.

8668

8671

8672

8673

8674

CHICAGOH!

8675

8678

8676

8679

8677

8680

8681

8682

8675 Von Photography
Designer: Jim Lienhart

8676 W. Clement Stone
Designer: Jim Lienhart

8677 Curtiss, Inc,
Designer: Jim Lienhart

8678 Stockyard Inn
Designer: Jim Lienhart

8679 International Typetronics
Designer: Jim Lienhart

8680 Chameleon Color Crafts
Designer: Jim Lienhart

8681 Reflections of You
Designer: Jim Lienhart

8682 Congregational Church of Glen Ellyn
Designer: Jim Lienhart

8683 Mutual Employment Inc.
Designer: Jim Lienhart

8683

me

8684

8687

8685

SAVINGS & LOAN NEWS

8688

8686

8689

8690

8691

8692

8693

8696

8694

8697

8695

8698

8699

8700

8693   Kollar Heinz, Inc.
       Designer: Jim Lienhart

8694   Photronic Typographers, Inc.
       Designer: Jim Lienhart

8695   Savings Institutions
       Designer: Jim Lienhart

8696   Series of Promotional Trademarks
          for Jim Lienhart
       Designer: Jim Lienhart

8697   Jim Lienhart
          (He's Honest)
       Designer: Jim Lienhart

8698   Jim Lienhart
          (He's Cuddly)
       Designer: Jim Lienhart

8699   Jim Lienhart
          (He's Patriotic)
       Designer: Jim Lienhart

8700   Jim Lienhart
          (He's Romantic)
       Designer: Jim Lienhart

8701

8703

8704

8702

8705

8706

8707

8708

8709

8701   Jim Lienhart
       (He's Debonair)
       Designer: Jim Lienhart

8702   Jim Lienhart
       (He's Emotional)
       Designer: Jim Lienhart

8703   Jim Lienhart
       (He's Athletic)
       Designer: Jim Lienhart

8704   Jim Lienhart
       (He's Creative)
       Designer: Jim Lienhart

8705   Jim Lienhart
       (He's Diligent)
       Designer: Jim Lienhart

8706   Hider Energy System, Inc.
       Designer: Lesniewicz/Navarre

8707   Libbey-Owens-Ford Co.
       Designer: Lesniewicz/Navarre

8708   Bailey
       Designer: Lesniewicz/Navarre

8709   SBS/Construction Management, Inc.
       Designer: Lesniewicz/ Navarre

8710

8714

8711

8715

"REACT"

8712

Glasfast

8716

8713

8717

BUR

8718

8719

8720

We Mean Business

8721

8710 Owens-Corning Fiberglas
Corporation
Designer: Lesniewicz/Navarre

8711 Owens-Corning Fiberglas
Corporation
Designer: Lesniewicz/Navarre

8712 Owens-Corning Fiberglas
Corporation
Designer: Lesniewicz/Navarre

8713 Owens-Corning Fiberglas
Corporation
Designer: Lesniewicz/Navarre

8714 Owens-Corning Fiberglas
Corporation
Designer: Lesniewicz/Navarre

8715 Owens-Corning Fiberglas
Corporation
Designer: Lesniewicz/Navarre

8716 Owens-Corning Fiberglas
Corporation
Designer: Lesniewicz/Navarre

8717 Owens-Corning Fiberglas
Corporation
Designer: Lesniewicz/Navarre

8718 Owens-Corning Fiberglas
Corporation
Designer: Lesniewicz/Navarre

8719 Owens-Corning Fiberglas
Corporation
Designer: Lesniewicz/ Navarre

8720 Owens-Corning Fiberglas
Corporation
Designer: Lesniewicz/Navarre

8721 Owens-Corning Fiberglas
Corporation
Designer: Lesniewicz/Navarre

8722

8726

8723

8727

8724

8728

8725

8729

8730

8731

8732

8733

8722	Owens-Illinois	Designer: Lesniewicz/Navarre
8723	Owens-Illinois	Designer: Lesniewicz/Navarre
8724	Owens-Illinois	Designer: Lesniewicz/Navarre
8725	Ritter	Designer: Lesniewicz/Navarre
8726	Mohon Realty	Designer: Lesniewicz/Navarre
8727	Mohon Realty	Designer: Lesniewicz/Navarre
8728	Mohon Realty	Designer: Lesniewicz/Navarre
8729	Bostleman Corporation	Designer: Lesniewicz/Navarre
8730	Dana/Spicer/Chelsea	Designer: Lesniewicz/Navarre
8731	Dana/Spicer/Chelsea	Designer: Lesniewicz/Navarre
8732	Dana/Spicer/Chelsea	Designer: Lesniewicz/Navarre
8733	Dana/Spicer/Chelsea	Designer: Lesniewicz/Navarre

8734

8738

8735

8739

8736

8740

8737

8741

8742

Westbrook
Apartments

8743

Camp Hemlock

8744

8745

8734   Vetus
Designer: Lesniewicz/Navarre

8735   Ursula Cauffiel School of Music
Designer: Lesniewicz/Navarre

8736   Tuschman Steel
Designer: Lesniewicz/Navarre

8737   The Toledo Museum of Art
Designer: Lesniewicz/Navarre

8738   Dunbar Mechanical
Designer: Lesniewicz/Navarre

8739   Gary Lesniewicz
Designer: Lesniewicz/Navarre

8740   Personal Touch
Designer: Lesniewicz/Navarre

8741   Elan Energy
Designer: Lesniewicz/Navarre

8742   Westbrook
Designer: Lesniewicz/Navarre

8743   Camp Hemlock
Designer: Lesniewicz/Navarre

8744   Gordon Grant
Designer: Lesniewicz/Navarre

8745   Professionel, Inc.
Designer: Lesniewicz/Navarre

8746

JIM**YARK**///////

8750

8747

8751

8748

COUNTRY
CLINIC
EQUINE

8752

8749

Finks
Fine
Foods

8753

8754

8755

8756

| 8746 | Jim Yark |
| | Designer: Lesniewicz/Navarre |

| 8747 | Professional Planning Services |
| | Designer: Lesniewicz/Navarre |

| 8748 | Country Equine |
| | Designer: Lesniewicz/Navarre |

| 8749 | Finks Fine Foods |
| | Designer: Lesniewicz/Navarre |

| 8750 | Jeff Fout Stables |
| | Designer: Lesniewicz/Navarre |

| 8751 | St. Lukes Hospital |
| | Designer: Lesniewicz/Navarre |

| 8752 | Toledo Popcorn Co. |
| | Designer: Lesniewicz/Navarre |

| 8753 | The Healthy Woman |
| | Designer: Lesniewicz/Navarre |

| 8754 | The French Bakery |
| | Designer: Lesniewicz/Navarre |

| 8755 | Jones & Henry |
| | Designer: Lesniewicz/Navarre |

| 8756 | Sunshine |
| | Designer: Lesniewicz/Navarre |

| 8757 | The Hair Depot |
| | Designer: Lesniewicz/Navarre |

8757

8758

8762

8759

8763

8760

8764

8761

8765

8766

8767

8768

8769

adventure shop

8770

8774

8771

8775

8772

8776

8773

8777

8778

8779

8780

8770   Giant Products Company
       Designer: Lesniewicz/Navarre

8771   Monroe Shock
       Designer: Lesniewicz/Navarre

8772   Solar Trucking Company
       Designer: Lesniewicz/Navarre

8773   Duquette Plumbing
       Designer: Lesniewicz/Navarre

8774   Suburban Showcase of Homes
       Designer: Lesniewicz/Navarre

8775   CEMA
       Designer: Lesniewicz/Navarre

8776   Kennecorp
       Designer: Lesniewicz/Navarre

8777   Planned Parenthood
       Designer: Lesniewicz/Navarre

8778   Deopke/Lesniewicz
       Designer: Lesniewicz/Navarre

8779   WGTE
       Designer: Lesniewicz/Navarre

8780   Fantacy Hill Farms Limited
       Designer: Lesniewicz/Navarre

8781

THE DOCKSIDE FISH COMPANY

8782

Loveladies Tennis Club

8783

TOT SPOT

8784

8785

ANNENBERG CINEMATHEQUE

8786

WALNUT STREET

8787

8788

8789

8790

8791

8781 The Dockside Fish Company
Designer: Kramer, Miller, Lomden,
Glassman

8782 Loveladies Tennis Club
Designer: Kramer, Miller, Lomden,
Glassman

8783 Tot Spot
Designer: Kramer, Miller, Lomden,
Glassman

8784 Bernard Toll
Designer: Kramer, Miller, Lomden,
Glassman

8785 Annenberg Cinematheque
Designer: Kramer, Miller,Lomden,
Glassman

8786 1608 Walnut Street
Designer: Kramer, Miller, Lomden,
Glassman

8787 Narco Scientific
Designer: Kramer, Miller, Lomden,
Glassman

8788 SMS
Designer: Kramer, Miller, Lomden,
Glassman

8789 Irene's Charcuterie
Designer: Kramer, Miller, Lomden.
Glassman

8790 Ristorante DiLullo
Designer: Kramer, Miller, Lomden,
Glassman

8791 Philadalphia Martime Museum
Designer: Kramer, Miller, Lomden,
Glassman

8792

8795

gallllery

8793

8796

8794

8797

8798

8799

8800

8792   12 P.B.S.
       Designer: Kramer, Miller, Lomden,
       Glassman

8793   200 P
       Designer: Kramer, Miller, Lomden,
       Glassman

8794   Philadelphia Restaurant Festival
       Designer: Kramer, Miller, Lomden,
       Glassman

8795   Gallery 3
       Designer: Vincent J. Mielcarek

8796   Marina Cafe
       Designer: Vincent J. Mielcarek

8797   Moravian Florist
       Designer: Vincent J. Mielcarek

8798   Mutual Aid Project
       Designer: Vincent J. Mielcarek

8799   Falcon Design, LTD
       Designer: Vincent J. Mielcarek

8800   Staten Island Hospital
       Designer: Vincent J. Mielcarek

8801

8803

8802

8804

8805

8806

8807

8808

8801 Gateway State Bank
Designer: Vincent J. Mielcarek

8802 Terra Equities
Designer: Vincent J. Mielcarek

8803 Staten Island Botanical Garden
Designer: Vincent J. Mielcarek

8804 College Quest
Designer: Vincent J. Mielcarek

8805 Staten Island Zoo
Designer: Vincent J. Mielcarek

8806 Cortina Valley
Designer: Vincent J. Mielcarek

8807 New York City Builders Association
Designer: Vincent J. Mielcarek

8808 Our Saviour Lutheran Church
Designer: Vincent J. Mielcarek

8809

8811

TORWEST

8810

8812

GREGG

8813

VALMONT TRADE CENTER

8814

COLORADO ELECTRIC

8815

8809	Wagner College Designer: Vincent J. Mielcarek
8810	Classroom Consortia Media Designer: Vincent J. Mielcarek
8811	Torwest Designer: Carole Nervig
8812	Gregg Homes Inc. Designer: Carole Nervig
8813	Valmont Trade Center Designer: Carole Nervig
8814	Colorado Electric Designer: Carole Nervig
8815	Parkfield Designer: Carole Nervig
8816	Skylink Corporation Designer: Carole Nervig

8816

8818

8819

FIRST NATIONAL

8820

8821

8817   Thomas C.M., Inc.
          Designer: Carole Nervig

8818   Beef & Grain Restaurant
          Designer: Neal Peterson
             Daremus & Company

8819   First National Bank & Trust
             Company
          Designer: Neal Peterson
             Daremus & Company

8820   Mary's Market
          Designer: Carl White
             Doremus & Company

8821   Communique
          Designer: Carl White
             Doremus & Company

8822

Whittier Inc.

8826

SUPRACOTE

8823

 CHICAGOLAND FEDERAL SAVINGS

8824

8827

8825

8828

Charles E. Hackett & Co.

8830

8831

Flagg Industries, Inc.

8822 Whittier Inc.
Designer: Carl White
Doremus & Company

8823 Chicago Federal Savings
Designer: Carl White
Doremus & Company

8824 The Henderson Company
Designer: Carl White
Doremus & Company

8825 Superior Optical Company
Designer: Ray Engle & Associates

8826 Supracote
Designer: Ray Engle & Associates

8827 Photography West
Designer: Ray Engle & Associates

8828 Marcy
Designer: Ray Engle & Associates

8829 Charles E. Hackett & Co.
Designer: Ray Engle & Associates

8830 Caravelle Communities
Designer: Ray Engle & Associates

8831 Flag Industries, Inc.
Designer: Ray Engle & Associates

8832

8835

8833

8836

8834

8837

8839

8840

8832 Pharmasea Services
Designer: Ray Engle & Associates

8833 Home Energy Survey
Designer: Ray Engle & Associates

8834 Architectural Graphics
Designer: Ray Engle & Associates

8835 International Electronic
        Research Corp.
Designer: Ray Engle & Associates

8836 Pala Mesa
Designer: Ray Engle & Associates

8837 Diamond Perforated Metals, Inc.
Designer: Ray Engle & Associates

8838 Woodland Grove
Designer: Ray Engle & Associates

8839 Wood Lighting Industries
Designer: Ray Engle & Associates

8840 Max Factor
Designer: Ray Engle & Associates

8841

8844

8842

8845

8843

8846

8847

HALLMARK PRODUCTIONS

8848

8849

8841   Seader, Inc.
Designer: Ray Engle & Associates

8842   Aliso Hills
Designer: Ray Engle & Associates

8843   Cooper Communications
Designer: Ray Engle & Associates

8844   California Apple Advisory Board
Designer: Ray Engle & Associates

8845   Reliance Steel Company
Designer: Ray Engle & Associates

8846   Sea World
Designer: Ray Engle & Associates

8847   Hallmark Productions
Designer: Ray Engle & Associates

8848   Ernest W. Hahn
Designer: Ray Engle & Associates

8849   Westaire Publishing
Designer: Ray Engle & Associates

8850

8853

8851

8854

8852

8855

8856

8857

8858

8859

8860

8861

PRISMATONE

8865

8862

8866

8863

LE SOIE
BOUTIQUE

8867

8864

8868

8869

 FESTIN

8870

8871

 CORTINA BIENES RAICES

8872

8876

MANN
BROTHERS

8877

The New
Wreckers
Lounge

8873

GOOD SHEPHERD
MEDICAL CENTER

8874

SOUTHLAND
MORTGAGE
CORPORATION

8878

GENESIS
BREAST DIAGNOSTIC CENTER

8875

CALAIS VILLAS

First Capital Companies

8879

8880

8881

8882

8886

FINSBURY POINTE

T O W N H O U S E S

8883

8887

8884

8888

ASPEN·LTD

8885

8889

South Florida Group Health

8890

8891

8882   Willow Creek Condominiums
        Designer: Horwitz, Mann
            & Bukvic, Inc.

8883   Cincinnati Suburban Press, Inc.
        Designer: Horwitz, Mann
            & Bukvic, Inc.

8884   Florence Bowl
        Designer: Horwitz, Mann
            & Bukvic, Inc.

8885   Washington Federals (USFL)
        Designer: Horwitz, Mann
            & Bukvic, Inc.

8886   Finsbury Pointe Condominiums
        Designer: Horwitz, Mann
            & Bukvic, Inc.

8887   Alexander's Floral Shoppes
        Designer: Horwitz, Mann
            & Bukvic, Inc.

8888   Aspen, Ltd.
        Designer: Horwitz, Mann
            & Bukvic, Inc.

8889   South Florida Group Health
        Designer: Young & Martin Design

8890   Sandy Springs Minor Emergency
            Medical Center
        Designer: Young & Martin Design

8891   Contract Grass, Inc.
        Designer: Young & Martin Design

8892

8895

8893

AmeriHealth

8896

8894

Where good things develop fast.

8898

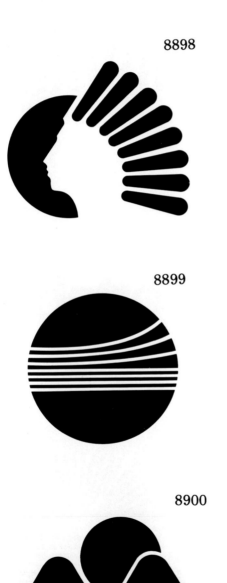

8899

8900

8892 R & R Evaluations, Inc.
      Designer: Young & Martin Design

8893 AmeriHealth, Inc.
      Designer: Young & Martin Design

8894 Associated Regional Accounting
         Firms
      Designer: Young & Martin Design

8895 Native Tree, Inc.
      Designer: Young & Martin Design

8896 Young & Martin Design
      Designer: Young & Martin Design

8897 Jack Rabbit Film Processing
      Designer: Harvey Dellinger

8898 Tomichi Condominiums
      Designer: Harvey Dellinger

8899 Graphics Now
      Designer: Harvey Dellinger

8900 Mountain Horizons Condominiums
      Designer: Harvey Dellinger

8901

8904

8902

8905

portables

8903

8906

Morehead Shores

8907

8908

8909

8910

8901 Four Oaks
      Designer: Harvey Dellinger

8902 Forthill
      Designer: Harvey Dellinger

8903 Structural Concepts
      Designer: Paul Frick Graphic Design

8904 High Museum Gift Shop
      Designer: Paul Frick Graphic Design

8905 Portables, Inc.
      Designer: Paul Frick Graphic Design

8906 Venture Management, Inc.
      Designer: Paul Frick Graphic Design

8907 WOWI Radio Station
      Designer: Everett Forbes

8908 Colonial Institute For Child and
          Adolesent Psychiatry
      Designer: Everett Forbes

8909 Women's Health Forum
      Designer: Everett Forbes

8910 Patrick Henry Hospital
      Designer: Everett Forbes

8913

8911

8912

8914

GROUP FOUR
.4.
MAIL, INC.

15 EAST BETHPAGE RD.
516/752-7952
PLAINVIEW, N.Y. 11803
G.F.M. 1978

8915

8916

8917

8918

8919

8911   Worldwide Security Systems
Designer: Constance Kovar Graphic
Design, Inc.

8912   Atlantic Cable Television Publishing
Designer: Constance Kovar Graphic
Design, Inc.

8913   Ckarat Advertising
Designer: Constance Kovar Graphic
Design, Inc.

8914   Group Four Mail
Designer: Constance Kovar Graphic
Design, Inc.

8915   Ckat & Associates
Designer: Constance Kovar Graphic
Design, Inc.

8916   Massaro Corp Contractors
Designer: Adam, Filippo & Moran
Inc., Design Consultants

8917   Audio Visual Consultants
Designer: Adam, Filippo & Moran
Inc., Design Consultants

8918   Keystone Medical Equip. Corp Inc.
Designer: Adam, Filippo & Moran
Inc., Design Consultants

8919   Bar Restaurant
Designer: Adam, Filippo & Moran
Inc., Design Consultants

8920

300
Weyman
Plaza

8924

THIRTEEN
HUNDRED
NEW YORK
AVENUE

8921

8925

8922

Douglas
Municipal
Airport
Charlotte, N.C.

8926

LAND
SEA & AIR

DEVELOPMENT CORPORATION

8923

Allegheny
Center

8927

Three
Rivers
Computer

8928

Westinghouse
Credit
Corporation

8929

RKS INSTITUTE

8930

8920   Lucien Caste Architects
        Designer: Adam, Filippo & Moran
          Inc., Design Consultants

8921   Thompson Homes
        Designer: Adam, Filippo & Moran
          Inc., Design Consultants

8922   Douglas Municipal Airport
        Designer: Adam, Filippo & Moran
          Inc., Design Consultants

8923   Douglas Air
        Designer: Adam, Filippo & Moran
          Inc., Design Consultants

8924   DAON Corporation
        Designer: Adam, Filippo & Moran
          Inc., Design Consultants

8925   Jeaunette Glass
        Designer: Adam, Filippo & Moran
          Inc., Design Consultants

8926   Land, Sea, & Air
        Designer: Adam, Filippo & Moran
          Inc., Design Consultants

8927   Three Rivers Computer
        Designer: Adam, Filippo & Moran
          Inc., Design Consultants

8928   Westinghouse Credit Corporation
        Designer: Adam, Filippo & Moran
          Inc., Design Consultants

8929   RKS Institute
        Designer: Gina M. Palazzo

8930   Crisdel Construction Company
        Designer: Gina M. Palazzo

8931   JoAnn Palazzo, Exercise Physiologist
        Designer: Gina M. Palazzo

8931

JoAnn Palazz

8932

THE FIRST AGENCY

8936

Peg tight

8933

NARTA NEWS

8937

PB

Petrini

8934

Elmwood Park Plaza

8938

RS

8935

Foremost Corrugated
Company, Inc.

8939

Palazzo

8940

Fountain Hills
Heating & Cooling

8941

MOTECH

8942

Minner Realty

8932	The First Agency Insurance Designer: Gina M. Palazzo
8933	NARTA News Designer: Gina M. Palazzo
8934	Elmwood Park Plaza Designer: Gina M. Palazzo
8935	Foremost Corrugated Co., Inc. Designer: Gina M. Palazzo
8936	Pigtight (fictitious furniture product) Designer: Gina M. Palazzo
8937	Petrini Realty & Insurance Co. Designer: Gina M. Palazzo
8938	Robert E. Smith, Graphic Arts Designer: Gina M. Palazzo
8939	Palazzo Design Designer: Gina M. Palazzo
8940	F.H. Heating & Cooling Designer: Ron Matteson
8941	Scottsdale Public Schools Designer: Ron Matteson
8942	Minner Realty Designer: Ron Matteson
8943	Corporate Credit Union of Az Designer: Ron Matteson

8943

CORPORATE

8944

Classic Running Boards of Arizona

8948

8945

8949

8950

8946

8947

8951

employment consultants

8953

8954

gibbons·wilson·young

ADVERTISING   PUBLIC   RELATIONS INC.

8955

H·O·A·G·S
CATERING
SERVICE

8944   Classic Running Boards of Az
Designer: Ron Matteson

8945   Minner Realty
Designer: Ron Matteson

8946   Wallace Minner
Designer: Ron Matteson

8947   Minner Inc.
Designer: Ron Matteson

8948   Pro/Am Mini Sport Games
Designer: Ron Matteson

8949   Blox
Designer: Ron Matteson

8950   Earth Signs
Designer: Ron Matteson

8951   P.D.O.P.S.
Designer: Ron Matteson

8952   Employment Consultants
Designer: Ron Matteson

8953   Grafiks Two
Designer: Ron Matteson

8954   G.W. & Y. Advertising & p.r.
Designer: Ron Matteson

8955   Hoag's Catering Service
Designer: Lanny Sommese

8956

8960

8957

8961

8958

8962

8959

8963

8964

8965

8966

(.,:;'?"The)
LEMONT
GARAGE
GASOLINE
KEROSENE
AND SEC-
RETARIAL
SERVICES
(.,:;'"!*?-)

8967

8968

8972

8969

8973

8970

8974

8971

8975

8976

8977

8978

8979

8968   Garry McShea Construction Co.
        Designer: Lanny Sommese

8969   Garry McShea Construction Co.
            (proposed)
        Designer: Lanny Sommese

8970   Garry McShea Construction Co.
        Designer: Larry Sommese

8971   The Press Box
        Designer: Lanny Sommese

8972   Ralph Licastro
            (Proposed)
        Designer: Lanny Sommese

8973   Ralph Licastro
            (proposed)
        Designer: Lanny Sommese

8974   Ralph Licastro
            (proposed)
        Designer: Lanny Sommese

8975   Joel Confer
        Designer: Lanny Sommese

8976   Joel Confer
            (proposed)
        Designer: Lanny Sommese

8977   International Assurance, Inc.
        Designer: Izhar Zik

8978   Storm Opinion Center
        Designer: Izhar Zik

8979   Technics in Design
        Designer: Izhar Zik

8980

8984

8981

8985

8982

8986

8983

8987

8988

8989

8990

8991

8980   The Graphics Gourmet
Designer: Izhar Zik

8981   Atara Designs, Inc.
Designer: Izhar Zik

8982   Insurance Institute For Research
Designer: Izhar Zik

8983   In The Beginning
Designer: Izhar Zik

8984   Quick Test, Inc.
Designer: Izhar Zik

8985   Zik Jewelry
Designer: Izhar Zik

8986   Northern Nuts & Bolts Co.
Designer: Izhar Zik

8987   Dalia
Designer: Izhar Zik

8988   Homsi, Inc.
Designer: Izhar Zik

8989   Personal International Courier
Service
Designer: Izhar Zik

8990   ADM Industries, Inc.
Designer: Izhar Zik

8991   Interstate Planning Association
Designer: Izhar Zik

8992

8996

8993

LESNEY

ELECTRONICS

8997

8994

8998

8995

8999

O N — L I N E

9001

9002

9003

9004

interior impressions

9005

S Q U A R E
■ **ONE** ■
CONSTRUCTION

9006

CHAMBER OF **COMMERCE**
BRYAN / COLLEGE STATION, TX

9007

9008

COURTYARD
INTERIORS

9009

COURTYARD
ANTIQUES

9010

COURTYARD
GALLERY

9011

COURTYARD
CLASSICS

THE
DOCTOR'S
OFFICE
9012

acp 9013

down to **EARTH** 9014

9015

9004 Interior Impressions
Designer: Luis Gonzalez
Graphic Concepts

9005 Square One Construction
Designer: Luis Gonzalez
Graphic Concepts

9006 Bryan-College Station Chamber
of Commerce
Designer: Ron Martin
Graphic Concepts

9007 Texas Real Estate Research Center
Designer: Ron Martin
Graphic Concepts

9008 Courtyard Interiors
Designer: Celia Jeter
Graphic Concepts

9009 Courtyard Antiques
Designer: Celia Jeter
Graphic Concepts

9010 Courtyard Gallery
Designer: Celia Jeter
Graphic Concepts

9011 Courtyard Classics
Designer: Celia Jeter
Graphic Concepts

9012 The Doctor's Office
Designer: Celia Jeter
Graphic Concepts

9013 Athletic Computer Programs
Designer: Joni McGee
Graphic Concepts

9014 Down to Earth
Designer: Joe Denton
Graphic Concepts

9015 The Design Company
Designer: Bob Zarwell

9016

9020

9017

9021

9022

9018

9023

9019

9024

9025

9026

9027

9016   1976 Popai Exhibit
       Designer: Bob Zarwell

9017   Vulcan Industries Corporation
       Designer: Bob Zarwell

9018   Prestige Management Inc.
       Designer: Bob Zarwell

9019   Greater Milwaukee Open
       Designer: Bob Zarwell

9020   Institute of Health Management
       Designer: Bob Zarwell

9021   Funway Holidays
       Designer: Bob Zarwell

9022   Ridgeway Realty Inc.
       Designer: Bob Zarwell

9023   Midwest Business Brokers
       Designer: Bob Zarwell

9024   J-K Art Directions
       Designer: Bob Zarwell

9025   Americanway Carwash Systems Inc.
          (proposed)
       Designer: Bob Zarwell

9026   Line Tone Litho Inc.
       Designer: Bob Zarwell

9027   Kingshead Stylists
       Designer: Bob Zarwell

9028

9031

BOB ARWELL

ART FOR
ADVERTISING

784-5655

18120 MILWAUKEE AVE.
BROOKFIELD, WI
53005

CATS' PAJAMAS

9029

9032

9030

**WOMEN'S
INDEPENDENT
FILM
FESTIVAL
!**

OCTOBER 21-27, 1983
SUBURBAN WORLD THEATRE

9033

9034

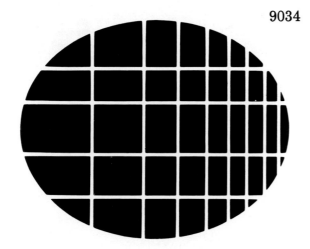

9028	Bob Zarwell Designer: Bob Zarwell
9029	Diversified Management Co. Designer: Cats' Pajamas
9030	Women's Independent Film Festival Designer: Cats' Pajamas
9031	Cats' Pajamas Designer: Cats' Pajamas
9032	Cooperating Fund Drive Designer: Cats' Pajamas
9033	Iris Video Designer: Cats' Pajamas
9034	EarthTech Designer: Valerie Kutchey
9035	TeleArts Designer: Valerie Kutchey
9036	The Westrend Group of the Trend Report Designer: P.J. Kelly

9035

9036

9041

9037

LEARNING

9042

9038

BLACK HAWK COUNTY ENERGY CONGRESS

9039

9043

9040

9044

9045

9046

9047

9048

9037   Learning Trends
       Designer: P.J. Kelly

9038   Interserv Management Services
       Designer: P.J. Kelly

9039   Peoples Mutual Savings and Loan
       Designer: Robert Hellman
          Hellman Design Assoc.,Inc.

9040   Champion Advertising
       Designer: Tom Roper
          Hellman Design Assoc., Inc.

9041   Tom R Roper
       Designer:Tom Roper
          Hellman Design Assoc., Inc.

9042   Black Hawk County Energy Congress
       Designer: Tom Roper
          Hellman Design Assoc., Inc.

9043   Schoenfeld Clinical Laboratory
       Designer: Kim Behm
          Hellman Design Assoc., Inc.

9044   Reed and Association
       Designer: Kim Behm
          Hellman Design Assoc., Inc.

9045   Jan Jacobson Photography
       Designer: Kim Behm
          Hellman Design Assoc., Inc.

9046   Hellman Design Associates, Inc.
       Designer: Gary Gersema
          Hellman Design Assoc., Inc.

9047   Technical Assistance Program
       Designer: Gary Gersema
          Hellman Design Assoc., Inc.

9048   Thermal Corporation
       Designer: Gary Gersema
          Hellman Design Assoc., Inc.

9049

9053

9050

9054

9051

9055

9052

9056

9057

9058

9059

9060

9049   First Holding Corporation
Designer: Gary Gersema
Hellman Design Assoc., Inc.

9050   Perpetual Savings and Loan Assoc.
Designer: Gary Gersema
Hellman Design Assoc., Inc.

9051   Walker's Water
Designer: Christopher C. Henneman

9052   Feminist Counselors
Designer: Christopher C. Henneman

9053   Retail Advertising Seminar 1982
Designer: Christopher C. Henneman

9054   Dominick Valenti
Designer: Christopher C. Henneman

9055   Christopher C. Henneman
Designer: Christopher C. Henneman

9056   Britton Racing Group
Designer: 5 Penguins Design, Inc.

9057   Chuck Alton Productions
Designer: 5 Penguins Design, Inc.

9058   Datatree
Designer: 5 Pengrins Design, Inc.

9059   California Fine Arts Atelier
Designer: 5 Penguins Design, Inc.

9060   Self Care Products, Inc.
Designer: 5 Penguins Design, Inc.

9061

9062

9064

9063

9065

The Left Bank

9066

9067

APTICK

9068

9069

NEWS

9070

9071

9074

9075

9072

9076

9073

9077

9078

9079

9080

9081

9070   Bechet's Restaurant Inc.
Designer: D. Bruce Zahor

9071   Pompizoo Restaurant
Designer: D. Bruce Zahor

9072   Jaqueline Smith, Ph. D.
Designer: D. Bruce Zahor

9073   New York City Housing
Development Corp.
Designer: D. Bruce Zahor

9074   Apple Bingo Supplies
Designer: D. Bruce Zahor

9075   "Selling Artist Materials "
A.J. Wildman & Son, Inc.
Designer: D. Bruce Zahor

9076   Grand Central Racquetball Club Inc.
Designer: D. Bruce Zahor

9077   Apro Systems Inc.
Designer: D. Bruce Zahor

9078   New York City Dep. of Parks
and Recreation
Designer: D. Bruce Zahor

9079   Leif Hope's Laundry Restaurant Inc.
Designer: D. Bruce Zahor

9080   Progressive Grocer Co.
Designer: D. Bruce Zahor

9081   Learning Resource Center, American
Express Co.
Designer: D. Bruce Zahor

9082

9086

9083

9087

9084

9088

9085

9089

9090

9091

Qually & Company, Inc

9092

9093

DAILYPLANET

9082 International Womens's Writing
Guild
Designer: D. Bruce Zahor

9083 "A Choice in Therapy" Inc.
Designer: D. Bruce Zahor

9084 The Learning Store Ltd.
Designer: D. Bruce Zahor

9085 Tenth House Enterprises Inc.
Designer: D. Bruce Zahor

9086 Command Travel Inc.
Designer: D. Bruce Zahor

9087 The Design Group, Inc.
D. Bruce Zahor

9088 Gambetta's Pizza
Designer: Gambetta-Bollmer
Graphic Design

9089 ASPEC Product Dev. Corp.
Designer: Gambetta-Bollmer
Graphic Design

9090 Cornell Forge Company
Designer: Robert Qually

9091 Qually & Company, Inc.
Designer: Robert Qually

9092 New Archery Products
Designer: Conrad Fialkowski

9093 Daily Planet
Designer: Conrad Fialdowski

9094

9097

9095

9094 (label appears with image)

Reruns

of San Francisco

9096

KINROW
ESTATES

9099

9100

9094 Olsen's Day Care Center
Designer: David Bullock

9095 Twin Jesters Restaurant
Designer: David Bullock

9096 Kinrow Estates
Designer: David Bullock

9097 R. Seth Vorisek
Designer: R. Seth Vorisek

9098 ReRuns of San Francisco
Designer: R. Seth Vorisek

9099 ReRuns of San Francisco
Designer: R. Seth Vorisek

9100 Peter Dechar
Designer: Tree Trapanese

9101 Chinese Christian Herald Crusades
Designer: Andy Lun

9102 Union Process, Inc.
Designer: P.R. Assoc., Inc.

9101

9102

9103

9107

CASHCO

9108

COMPUTER SHOWCASE

9104

ADA

9105

Olympia Centre

9109

WESTSIDE
COMMERCIAL BROKERAGE COMPANY

9110

KELLER

9106

DYNAQUEST

9112

WESTSIDE
T O W E R S

9113

Yarbrough
and company

9103 Metropolitan Hand Center
     Designer: Mary Beth Bostrum Cybul
        Hill and Knowlton, Inc.

9104 ADA
     Designer: Mary Beth Bostrum Cybul
        Hill and Knowlton, Inc.

9105 Olympia & York
     Designer: Mark Tendam
        Hill and Knowlton, Inc.

9106 Dynaquest
     Designer: Greg Scott
        Hill and Knowlton, Inc.

9107 Cashco
     Designer: Greg Scott
        Hill and Knowlton, Inc.

9108 Computer Showcase
     Designer: Phyllis Persechini
        Persechini & Moss

9109 Westside Commercial Brokerage Co.
     Designer: Phyllis Persechini
        Persechini & Moss

9110 Keller Construction Company
     Designer: Phyllis Persechini
        Persechini & Moss

9111 Young Musicians Foundation
     Designer: Shannon Heiman
        Persechini & Moss

9112 Westside Towers
     Designer: Shannon Heiman
        Persechini & Moss

9113 Yarbrough and Company
     Designer: Shannon Heiman
        Persechini & Moss

HOTEL BEL AIR SANDS

9116

9117

9114	Hotel Air Sands Designer: Shannon Heiman Persechini & Moss
9115	The Lone Ranger Designer: Shannon Heiman Persechini & Moss
9116	Giarnella Design Designer: Giarnella Design
9117	Graphic Dimensions Designer: Giarnella Design
9118	Graphic Dimensions Designer: Giarnella Design

9118

9119

9123

9120

9124

9121

9125

9122

912

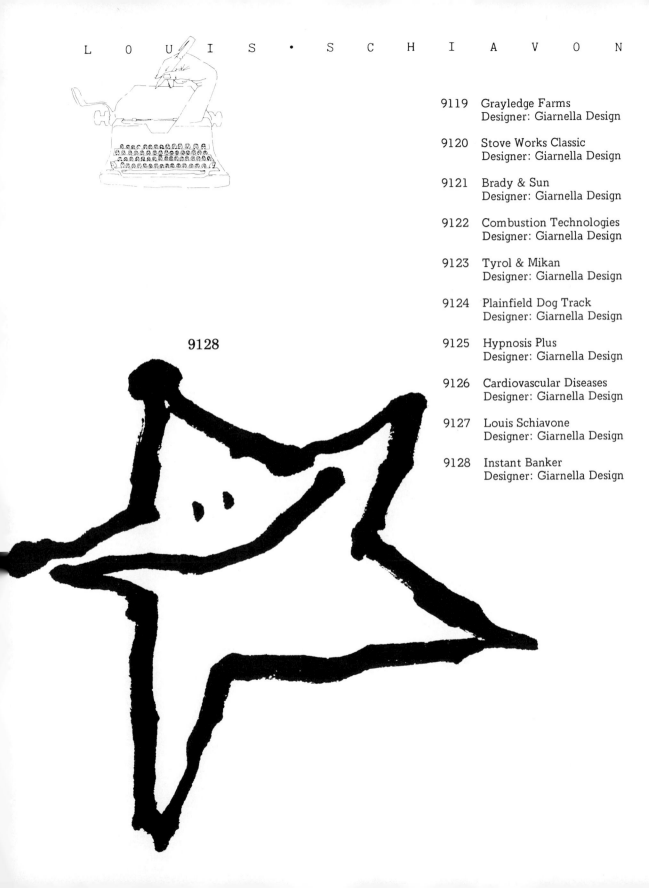

L O U I S • S C H I A V O N E

9128

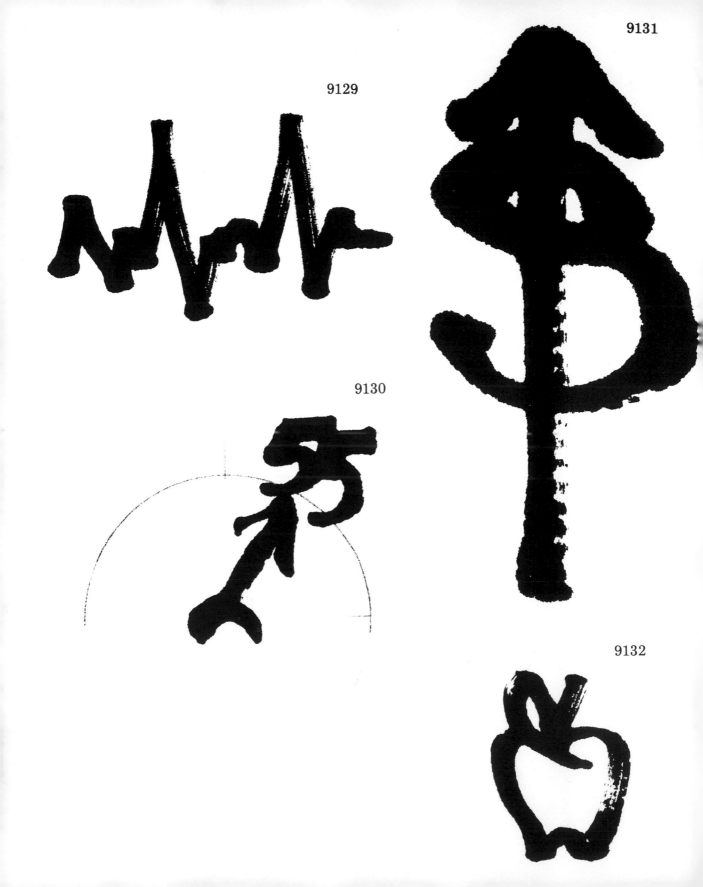

9129

9131

9130

9132

Advanced Group Life & Health Insurance

9134

9135

9129	Aetna Life and Casualty Co. Designer: Giarnella Design
9130	Aetna Life and Casualty Co. Designer: Giarnella Design
9131	Aetna Life and Casualty Co. Designer: Giarnella Design
9132	Aetna Life and Casualty Co. Designer: Giarnella Design
9133	Aetna Life and Casualty Co. Designer: Giarnella Design
9134	Aetna Life and Casualty Co. Designer: Giarnella Design
9135	Aetna Life and Casualty Co. Designer: Giarnella Design
9136	Aetna Life and Casualty Co. Designer: Giarnella Design
9137	Aetna Life and Casualty Co. Designer: Giarnella Casualty Co.

9136

9137

9138

9142

9139

9143

9140

9144

Hettig
& Company

9141

9145

9146

The Ashford Group, Inc.

9147

9148

9149

9138   H.A. Stroh Assoc., Inc.
       Designer: Stephen Longo & Assoc.

9139   Nabisco
       Designer: Stephen Longo & Assoc.

9140   Fersko, Wasilewski and Company
       Designer: Stephen Longo & Assoc.

9141   Stephen Longo
       Designer: Stephen Longo & Assoc.

9142   Nabisco
       Designer: Stephen Longo & Assoc.

9143   Gulf Houston Properties, Inc.
       Designer: Rosalie Ramsden

9144   Hettig & Co.
       Designer: Rosalie Ramsden

9145   YWCA of Houston
       Designer: Rosalie Ramsden

9146   The Ashford Group
       Designer: Rosalie Ramsden

9147   Professional Women in Agriculture
       Designer: Rosalie Ramsden

9148   The Museum of Printing History
       Designer: Rosalie Ramsden

9149   Astron Energy Corporation
       Designer: Scott Engen

9150

9154

9151

9155

9152

9156

9153

9157

9158

SPORTSAM

9159

**ROWMARK
SKI ACADEMY**

9160

SOLITUDE
SKI TEAM

9161

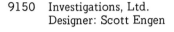

9150   Investigations, Ltd.
        Designer: Scott Engen

9151   Gamesman
        Designer: Scott Engen

9152   Childrens Dance Workshop
        Designer: Scott Engen

9153   Parking Services
        Designer: Scott Engen

9154   Printmakers
        Designer: Scott Engen

9155   Pens V
        Designer: Scott Engen

9156   K+K Medical Supply
        Designer: Scott Engen

9157   Associated Students of the
        University of Utah
        Designer: Scott Engen

9158   Sports Am
        Designer: Scott Engen

9159   Rowmark Ski Academy
        Designer: Scott Engen

9160   Solitude Ski Team
        Designer: Scott Engen

9161   Scott Engen, Ski Coach
        Designer: Scott Engen

9162

9166

9163

9167

9164

VINE·LORE

9168

PROJECT

DIÁLOGO

9165

9169

9170

9171

9162   Lone Peak Food and Beverage Inc.
Designer: Scott Engen

9163   Marcus Grant Advertising
Designer: Scott Engen

9164   Vine Lore
Designer: Scott Engen

9165   Creative Communications Consulting
Company
Designer: Scott Engen

9166   Graphic Concepts, Inc.
Designer: Scott Engen

9167   Lancaster Limited
Designer: Scott Engen

9168   Guadalupe Center of Salt Lake City
Designer: Scott Engen

9169   Diamond Tree Branch
Designer: Scott Engen

9170   Swiss Film Festival
Designer: Scott Engen

9171   Quadrant
Designer: Scott Engen

9172   International Applied Sciences Inc.
Designer: Benjamin R. Larrabee

9173   Damon Corporation
Designer: Benjamin R. Larrabee

9172

9173

9174

9178

9175

9179

9176

9180

9177

9181

9182

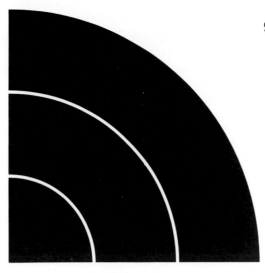

9174   Jerry Sharan Graphics
         Designer: Susanne Bordeau
         Jerry Sharan Graphics

9175   Arnold Peck Realty
         Designer: Susanne Bordeau
         Jerry Sharan Graphics

9176   Aviation Training Services
         Designer: Susanne Bordeau
         Jerry Sharan Graphics

9177   Pilot Proficiency Examiners
         Association, Inc.
         Designer: Jerry Sharan
         Sharan Graphics

9178   Mid-American Dance Company
         Designer: Dennis Ichiyama

9179   University Design Organization
         (proposal)
         Designer: Dennis Ichiyama

9180   The Monet Trio
         Designer: Dennis Ichiyama

9181   Weidlinger Associates
         Designer: George Tscherny

9182   Montgomery Communications, Inc.
         Designer: George Tscherny

9183   The Light Opera of Manhattan
         Designer: George Tscherny

9184   Ernst & Whinney
         Designer: George Tscherny

9183

9184

9185

9188

9186

9189

Greystone

9187

9190

9191

9192

9193

9185   Bender Management Consultants Inc.
       Designer: George Tscherny

9186   Fidelity Group of Funds
       Designer: George Tscherny

9187   Roto-Rooter
       Designer: George Tscherny

9188   SEi Trust Funds
       Designer: George Tscherny

9189   Greystone
       Designer: Jean-Claude Muller
          John Follis & Assoc.

9190   Dharmala
       Designer: Jean-Claude Muller
          John Follis & Assoc.

9191   Gajah Mada Plaza
       Designer: Joe Stoddard
          John Follis & Assoc.

9192   Converse Davis Dixon
       Designer: Joe Stoddard
          John Follis & Assoc.

9193   Panda Inn
       Designer: Connie Beck

9194

9198

9195

 RALPH HAHN AND ASSOCIATES
CONSULTING AND DESIGN ENGINEERS INC.

9199

ANDREWS ENVIRONMENTAL
ENGINEERING INC.

9196

Illinois
Department of
Revenue

9200

the
Graduat
School
of
Hair
Design

9197

Illinois
State Board of
Education

92

Koke Mil

9202

Citizens
Savings and Loan
Association

9203

9204

9205

9194   Springfield Mutual Realtors
        Designer: Com Unigraph Inc.

9195   Ralph Hahn and Associates
        Designer: Con Unigraph Inc.

9196   Illinois Department of Revenue
        Designer: Com Unigraph Inc.

9197   Illinois State Board of Education
        Designer: Com Unigraph Inc.

9198   St. Nicholas Apartments
        Designer: Com Unigraph Inc.

9199   Andrews Environmental
            Engineering Inc.
        Designer: Com Unigraph Inc.

9200   The Graduate School of Hair Design
        Designer: Com Unigraph Inc.

9201   Kokemill Development
        Designer: Com Unigraph Inc.

9202   Citizens Savings and Loan Assoc.
        Designer: Com Unigraph Inc.

9203   Springfield Central Area
            Development Association
        Designer: Com Unigraph Inc.

9204   BiPetro
        Designer: Com Unigraph Inc.

9205   Lithocrest Printing
        Designer: Com Unigraph Inc.

CONVOCOM

M.G. Nelson
Builder / Developer / Realtor

St. Mary's Hospital

 Firstbank of Illinois Co.

9210

 Dixon Bretscher Noonan, Inc.

9211

9206   Convocom Telecommunications
       Designer: Com Unigraph Inc.

9207   M.G. Nelson
       Designer: Com Unigraph Inc.

9208   St. Mary's Hospital
       Designer: Com Unigraph Inc.

9209   Firstbank of Illinois Co.
       Designer: Com Unigraph Inc.

9210   Dixon Bretscher Noonan, Inc.
       Designer: Com Unigraph Inc.

9211   Lincolnfest
       Designer: Com Unigraph Inc.

9212   St. Joseph's Hospital
       Designer: Com Unigraph Inc.

9212

 St Joseph's Hospital

9213

9217

9214

9218

PENGUIN·PRODUCTIONS

9215

9219

Goodies

9216

9220

The Ultimate Street Skate

9221

9222

9223

9224

9213   Forever Toys
        Designer: Bill Kinser
          Bill Kinser Design

9214   Intervalley Systems
        Designer: Bill Kinser
          & Lanny Sommese
          Lanny Sommese Design & Illus.

9215   Dante's Restaurants Inc.
        Designer: Lanny Sommese

9216   THOTS
        Designer: Ron Pierce

9217   Doctor's House Call For Pets
        Designer: Michael Faye

9218   Penguin Productions
        Designer: Michael Faye

9219   Goodties Shoelaces
        Designer: Michael Faye

9220   The Ultimate Street Skate
        Designer: Michael Faye

9221   Hot Stuff Shampoo
        Designer: Michael Faye

9222   Reruns For Little Ones
        Designer: Michael Faye

9223   Goochi Goo Children's Clothing
        Designer: Michael Faye

9224   Murphy Roth Interior Design
        Designer: Michael Faye

9225

9229

9226

9230

9227

9231

9228

9232

9233

9234

EVER GREEN

9235

9236

9240

YOUTH THEATRE GUILD

9237

9241

ALBERT MARDIKIAN
ENGINEERING

9238

9242

RADIANCE

9239

9243

EXECUTIVE COACHCRAFT

9245

9246

CANTERBURY INN

9247

9236	Solargas Designer: Michael Faye
9237	Chef's Pollo Designer: Michael Faye
9238	Cosmetic Development Systems Designer: Michael Faye
9239	Karlyn International Designer: Michael Faye
9240	Youth Theatre Guild Designer: Michael Faye
9241	Albert Mardikian Engineering Designer: Michael Faye
9242	Linda Staehr Designer: Michael Faye
9243	Worlds of Tile Designer: Michael Faye
9244	Executive Coachcraft, Inc. Designer: Michael Faye
9245	Sierra Spas Designer: Michael Faye
9246	Canterbury Inn Designer: Michael Faye
9247	The Glass Eye, Inc. Designer: Michael Faye

9248

9252

9249

9253
Coburn Consultants Inc

9250

925~

9251

925

9256

Manhattan Beach Education Foundation

9257

9258

9259

9248	Music and Memories	Designer: Michael Faye
9249	California Hi Lites	Designer: Michael Faye
9250	California Mint	Designer: Michael Faye
9251	Gerold & Mills Real Estate	Designer: Michael Faye
9252	California Optics	Designer: Michael Faye
9253	Coburn Consultants, Inc.	Designer: Michael Faye
9254	Cal Pacific Eyewear	Designer: Michael Faye
9255	The Porthole Restaurant	Designer: Michael Faye
9256	Manhattan Beach Education Foundation	Designer: Michael Faye
9257	Manhattan Beach Chamber of Commerce	Designer: Michael Faye
9258	National Healthcare Center	Designer: Michael Faye
9259	Family Health Centers	Designer: Michael Faye

9260

9264

9261

9265

TECHNOLOGY
SYSTEMS
ORGANIZATION
INC.

9262

9266

9263

9267

9268

9269

9260	Silver Shear Hair Design Designer: Michael Faye
9261	Computers, Et Cetera Designer: Michael Faye
9262	Republic Distributors, Inc. Designer: Machael Faye
9263	Hope Chapel Designer: Michael Faye
9264	Quoin Development Corp. Designer: Michael Faye
9265	Technology Systems Organization, Inc. Designer: Michael Faye
9266	Hook City Records Designer: Michael Faye
9267	Marquee Productions Designer: Michael Faye
9268	Anny's Hair Salon Designer: Michael Faye
9269	Palos Verdes Flooring Center Designer: Michael Faye
9270	Ascot Grand Prix Designer: Michael Faye

9270

Micro Linear

9271

RED COACH

9275

9272

ZURICLE

9276

MARKETING INC.

9273

9277

Westminster Software

9274

MMB

9278

GENESIS GROUP

Adventist Health System

9280

COLUMBIA DIVERSIFIED ENERGIES, inc.

9281

9282

Professional Athletes Career Enterprises, Inc.

9271 Micro Linear
Designer: Patty Richmond Design

9272 B & B Photography
Designer: Patty Richmond Design

9273 Fresh Western, Inc.
Designer: Patty Richmond Design

9274 McMillan, Moore, & Bucannan
Real Estate
(proposal)
Designer: Patty Richmond Design

9275 Bruce Church, Inc.
Designer: Patty Richmond Design

9276 Auricle
Designer: Patty Richmond Design

9277 Westminster Software
Designer: Patty Richmond Design

9278 Genesis Group
Designer: Patty Richmond Design

9279 Adventist Health System
Designer: Curt Hamilton
Robert Brandt Advertising, Inc.

9280 Columbia Diversified Energies, Inc.
Designer: Curt Hamilton
Robert Brandt Advertising, Inc.

9281 Lakeside Steel Corporation
Designer: Curt Hamilton
Robert Brandt Advertising, Inc.

9282 Professional Athletes Career
Enterprises, Inc.
Designer: Curt Hamilton
Robert Brandt Advertising, Inc.

9283

Hyde Park
Community Hospital

9284

THOREK
Hospital and
Medical Center

9287

9285

Glendale
Heights
Community
Hospital, Inc.

9288

the
WOOD
SPECIALISTS

9286

Garvey
Marketing
Group

9289

NEW DAY™

CENTER
SUBSTANCE ABUSE SERVICES

9290

9291

9292

9283   Hyde Park Community Hospital
      Designer: Waldo Pacheco
        Robert Brandt Advertising. Inc.

9284   Thorek Hospital and Medical Center
      Designer: Waldo Pacheco
        Robert Brandt Advertising, Inc.

9285   Glendale Heights Community
        Hospital
      Designer: Waldo Pacheco
        Robert Brandt Advertising, Inc.

9286   Garvey Marketing Group
      Designer: Waldo Pacheco
        Robert Brandt Advertising, Inc.

9287   Good Deal & Co.
      Designer: Waldo Pacheco
        Robert Brandt Advertising, Inc.

9288   The Wood Specialists
      Designer: Waldo Pacheco
        Robert Brandt Advertising, Inc.

9289   New Day Centers
      Designer: Cynthia Radke
        Robert Brandt Advertising, Inc.

9290   The Pointe
      Designer: Ron Spielman
        Robert Brandt Advertising, Inc.

9291   John H. Harland Co.
      Designer: John H. Harland Co.

9292   Harland Planning Meeting
      Designer: John H. Harland Co.

9293   Skyview Graphics, Inc.
      Designer: Constance Kovar Graphic
        Design, Inc.

9293

9294

9295

Baker's Dozen

warm, shaped cookies

9297

9296

Circular Screen

9298

BROADCASTERS MEDIA SERVICES, INC.

9299

9300

9301

9294 David Parker
      Designer: David Alexander Parker

9295 Baker's Dozen
      Designer: John K. Landis Graphic
          Design

9296 Circular Screen
      Designer: John K. Landis Graphic
          Design

9297 Sue Lindsey
      Designer: leAd Advertising & Design

9298 Potomac Inc.
      Designer: leAd Advertising & Design

9299 DRP Litho
      Designer: leAd Advertising & Design

9300 McArthur, Thomas
      Designer: leAd Advertising & Design

9301 Dave Rosencrans
      Designer: Mark Setteducatl Design

9302 John Battenberg
      Designer: Linda Fillhardt

9302

BATTENBERG

9303

9307

INA CORPORATION

9304

THE BIRTH
AND
FAMILY CENTER

9308

GANNETT

9305

9306

9309

CREAM OF WHEAT

9311

CHICOPEE

9303	DD Associates Designer: Linda Fillhardt
9204	The Birth & Family Center Designer: Linda Fillhardt
9305	Air National Designer: Linda Fillhardt
9306	Holmes & Company Designer: Linda Fillhardt
9307	INA Corporation Designer: Yasumura/CYB
9308	Gannett Designer: Yasumura/CYB
9309	Dannon Designer: Yasumura/CYB
9310	Cream of Wheat Designer: Yasumura/ CYB
9311	Chicopee Designer: Yasumura/CYB
9312	USA Today Designer: Yasumura/CYB

9312

USA TODAY

9313

WESTON

9314

9317

9315

9318

9316

9319

9320

9321

9322

9313	Weston Instruments Designer: Yasumura/CYB
9314	Uniting Community Church Designer: Maria Mazzara
9315	Design Group M Designer: Maria Mazzara
9316	Electron Optics Designer: Maria Mazzara
9317	City of South St. Paul Designer: Maria Mazzara
9318	JoAnn Nicholson & Judy Lewis Designer: Maria Mazzara
9319	Maria Mazzara Designer: Maria Mazzara
9320	Central Security Insurance Designer: Maria Mazzara
9321	Mark Kawell Designer: Maria Mazzara
9322	Minnesota Pollution Control Agency Designer: Maria Mazzara
9323	Winston Press Designer: Maria Mazzara

9323

9324

studio graphics

9328

9325

9329

SMSC

9326

9330

PERSIMMON PRODUCTIONS

9327

PROFESSIONAL · DEVELOPMENT · PROGRAMS

9331

· DESIGN · EAST · INC ·

9332

9333

9334

9335

9324 Studio Graphics
      Designer: Maria Mazzara

9325 Buck Hill Ski Racing Club
      Designer: Maria Mazzara

9326 Buck Hill Ski Racing Club
      Designer: Maria Mazzara

9327 Professional Development Programs
      Designer: Maria Mazzara

9328 Buckley's Ski Emporium
      Designer: Maria Mazzara

9329 Southwest Minnesota State College
      Designer: Maria Mazzara

9330 Persimmon Productions
      Designer: Maria Mazzara

9331 Design East
      Designer: Maria Mazzara

9332 Lindwood Forest Townhouses
      Designer: Maria Mazzara

9333 des Tasses Mug Shop
      Designer: Maria Mazzara

9334 Sandpebbles Gift Store
      Designer: Maria Mazzara

9335 American Israel Cultural Foundation
      Designer: Nanette Hucknall

9336

9337

9339

9338

9340

9341

9342

9336 Women's Networking Committee
      UJA-Federation Campaign
      Designer: Nanette Hucknall

9337 The Jewish Theological Seminary
      of America
      Designer: Nanette Hucknall

9338 Jewish Reconstructionist Foundation
      Designer: Nanette Hucknall

9339 Eurocom
      Designer: Marvin Trull

9340 Veshima Coffee Co. Ltd.
      Designer: Jitsuo Hoashi

9343

9341 Ness Tory Travel Club
      Designer: George McGinnis/
      David Parker

9342 Image Network
      Designer: George McGinnis/
      Susan Borgen

9343 Best Boy Feature Film
      Designer: George McGinnis/
      Lisa LLoyd

9344 WGN
      Designer: John Rea/
      George McGinnis

9344

9345

you're gonna
FALL FOR US

9349

9346

WGN

9350

You Should
See Us
Now

9347

11 Alive

9351

THE
DEAD
ZONE

9348

SHOWTIME'S
Astrology
T·O·D·A·Y

9352

9353

9354

9355

Middle East Television

9356

9345 WGN
Designer: John Rea/
George McGinnis

9346 WGN
Designer: John Rea/
George McGinnis

9347 WPIX New York
Designer: John Rea/
George McGinnis

9348 Showtime Entertainment
Designer: John Rea/
George McGinnis

9349 Channel 25 Boston
Designer: John Rea/
George McGinnis

9350 Channel 25 Boston
Designer: John Rea/
George McGinnis

9351 Paramount Pictures
Designer: John Rea/
George McGinnis

9352 Showtime Entertainment
Designer: George McGinnis

9353 Showtime Entertainment
Designer: George McGinnis

9354 T.V. Radio Caracas
Designer: George McGinnis

9355 Christian Broadcasting Television
Designer: George McGinnis

9356 Institute of French Petroleum
Designer: George McGinnis

9357

9361

9358

9362

9359

9363

9360

9364

9365

9366

9367

9357 Corinthian Broadcasting Corporation
Designer: George McGinnis

9358 Corinthian Broadcasting Corporation
Designer: George McGinnis

9359 Corinthian Broadcasting Corporation
Designer: George McGinnis

9360 Corinthian Broadcasting Corporation
Designer: George McGinnis

9361 Japan Chemical Shoes Industry
Association Inc.
Designer: Jitsuo Hoashi

9362 The Seiyu Stores Co. Limited
Designer: Jitsuo Hoashi

9363 Club "E" Nightclub
Designer: Jitsuo Hoashi

9364 Grouse Run, Inc.
Designer: Jitsuo Hoashi

9365 Les Halles
Designer: Jitsuo Hoashi

9366 Reduta Deux Theatrical Co.
Designer: Jitsuo Hoashi

9367 Fashion Store "Zero One"
Designer: Jitsuo Hoashi

9368 Art Directors Club
Designer: Jitsuo Hoashi

9368

9369

9373

9370

9374

9371

9375

9372

9376

9377

9378

9379

9380

9369   Christian Broadcasting Network
       Designer: Jitsuo Hoashi

9370   Veshima Coffee Co.
       Designer: Jitsuo Hoashi

9371   Morozoff Limited
       Designer: Jitsuo Hoashi

9372   Sutton Creek Partnership
       Designer: Wayne Kosterman
          Assoc., Inc.

9373   Saint Joseph Hospital
       Designer: Wayne Kosterman
          Assoc., Inc.

9374   Premier Banks, Inc.
       Designer: Wayne Kosterman
          Assoc., Inc.

9375   La Leche League International
       Designer: Wayne Kosterman
          Assoc., Inc.

9376   Minor Emergency Centers, Inc.
       Designer: Wayne Kosterman
          Assoc., Inc.

9377   Americor Enterprises, Inc.
       Designer: Wayne Kosterman
          Assoc., Inc.

9378   School District 54
       Designer: Wayne Kosterman
          Assoc., Inc.

9379   Bolingbrook Medical Center
       Designer: Wayne Kosterman
          Assoc., Inc.

9380   Village of Roselle
       Designer:Wayne Kosterman
          Assoc., Inc.

9381

9382

9383

9384

QUIKFENCE

LELAND MUSIC

9385

9386

9381	Alpha Graphix Designer: The Weller Institute
9382	Quickfence Designer: The Weller Institute
9383	Studio International Designer: The Weller Institute
9384	Leland Music Designer: The Weller Institute
9385	Dentsu, Inc. Designer: H.L. Chu & Co. Ltd.
9386	The Cooper Union Designer: H.L. Chu & Co. Ltd.
9387	Heather Evans Incorporated Designer:H.L. Chu & Co. Ltd.

9387

9388

9390

9389

9391

9392

9393

9394

9388 Winsor Dental Studio
Designer: H.L. Chu & Co. Ltd.

9389 New York University Medical Center
Blood Program
Designer: H.L.Chu & Co. Ltd.

9390 Pellegrini & Kaestle, Inc.
Designer: H.L. Chu & Co. Ltd.

9391 Press Brenner Communications, Inc.
Designer: H.L. Chu & Co.
Designer: H.L. Chu & Co. Ltd.

9392 Sun Tours Inc.
Designer: H.L.Chu & Co. Ltd.

9393 A.L. Havens Securities, Inc.
Designer: H.L. Chu & Co. Ltd

9394 Polk's Hobbies
Designer: H.L. Chu & Co. Ltd.

9395 Hoi Ling Chu
Designer: H.L. Chu & Co. Ltd.

9395

9396

9401

9397

9402

9398

9403

9399

9404

9400

9405

9406

9407

9408

9409

9396   Equestrian Centers of America, Inc.
Designer: Rose Farber

9397   Elaine Goldy Properties
Designer: Rose Farber

9398   San Fernando Community
Designer: Rose Farber

9399   BBC International
Designer: Rose Farber

9400   Western Technologies, Inc.
Designer: Rose Farber

9401   Aspen Hill
Designer: Rose Farber

9402   First Capital Partners, Inc.
Designer: Rose Farber

9403   Brentwood Energy
Designer: Rose Farber

9404   The Crystal Fountain Restaurant
Designer: Rose Farber

9405   Century General Corporation
Designer: Rose Farber

9406   Camseal Inc.
Designer: Rose Farber

9407   Sunset Summit Condominiums
Designer: Rose Farber

9408   American Capital Investors, Inc.
Designer: Rose Farber

9409   Corsair Asset Management, Inc.
Designer: Rose Farber

9410

9413

9411

9414

9412

9415

9416

9417

9410	Balloons Instead	Designer: Eugene Cheltenham
9411	California Mart	Designer: Eugene Cheltenham
9412	Spectra Star Kites	Designer: Eugene Cheltenham
9413	Sun King	Designer: Eugene Cheltenham
9414	Right Side of the Brain/Seminar	Designer: Eugene Cheltenham
9415	Skatey's	Designer: Eugene Cheltenham
9416	California Mart	Designer: Eugene Cheltenham
9417	Literary Women	Designer: Eugene Cheltenham
9418	Jack Loeb Printing Production	Designer: Eugene Cheltenham
9419	Kendra Kollectables	Designer: Eugene Cheltenham

9418

9419

9420

TM

9421

9422

9420 Games of the XXIII Olympiad
Los Angeles 1984
Designer: Robert Miles Runyan
& Associates

9421 Southern California Savings
Designer: Robert Miles Runyan
& Associates

9422 SARSA
Designer: Robert Miles Runyan
& Associates

9423 Obunsha Publishing Co., Ltd.
Designer: Robert Miles Runyan
& Associates

9423

9424

UNIBANCO

9427

VUARNET
FRANCE

9425

LOS · VAQUEROS

9428

9426

LOS · COYOTES

9429

9430

9431

9432

9424   Unibanco, S.A.
Designer: Robert Miles Runyan
& Associates

9425   Los Coyotes Country Club
Designer: Robert Miles Runyan
& Associates

9426   Los Coyotes Country Club
Designer: Robert Miles Runyan
& Associates

9427   Vuarnet France
Designer: Robert Miles Runyan
& Associates

9428   Visual Marketing Associates
Designer: Robert Miles Runyan
& Associates

9429   Pharmavite
Designer: Robert Miles Runyan
& Associates

9430   Jerry Pavey Design
Designer: Jerry Pavey Design

9431   Nancy Barchas
Designer: Jerry Pavey Design

9432   Federal Farm Credit Board
Designer: Jerry Pavey Design

9433

COMMUNICATORS ORIENTATION
WASHINGTON, DC

9437

9434

The 25th
Anniversary
Federal Farm
Credit Board

9438

Tia Queta

9435

9439

9436

Quarterly
The Fiscal Agency Of The Farm
Credit Banks
Review

9440

TEAMWORK: NOW, TOMORROW

9241

9442

9443

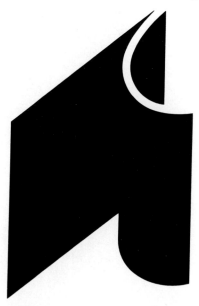

9433 Farm Credit Administration
      Designer: Jerry Pavey Design

9434 Federal Farm Credit Board
      Designer: Jerry Pavey Design

9435 Farm Credit Administration
      Designer: Jerry Pavey Design

9436 The Fiscal Agency for the
         Farm Credit Board
      Designer: Jerry Pavey Design

9437 Federal Farm Credit Board
      Designer: Jerry Pavey Design

9438 Tia Queta Mexican Restaurant
      Designer: Jerry Pavey Design

9439 Svec/ Conway Printers
      Designer: Jerry Pavey Design

9440 The American Institute
         of Cooperation
      Designer: Jerry Pavey Design

9441 Arntz Cobra
      Designer: Marty Neumeier

9442 Summit University
      Designer: Marty Neumeier

9443 Avant Cards
      Designer: Marty Neumeier

9444

9447

9445

9448

9446

9449

9450

9444 Educational Video
Designer: Marty Neumeier

9445 Chroma Litho
Designer: Marty Neumeier

9446 Paperbooks, Inc.
Designer: Marty Neumeier
& Kathleen Trainor Joynes

9447 Kings West
Designer: Marty Neumier
& Byron Glaser

9448 Western Medical
Designer: Marty Neumeier

9449 Creative Education
Designer: Marty Neumeier

9450 U.S. Invest
Designer: Marty Neumeier
& Sandra Higashi

9451 Edward deBono School of Thinking
Designer: Marty Neumeier

9452 Eatz Restaurants
Designer: Marty Neumeier

9451

9452

9453

9457

9454

9458

9455

9459

9456

9460

9461

9462

9463

9464

9453   Casper Events Center
        Designer: Communication Arts Inc.

9454   Medical Management Group
        Designer: Communication Arts Inc.

9455   Babiyar Park
        Designer: Communication Arts Inc.

9456   Monitor Maintenance
        Designer: Communication Arts Inc.

9457   Champion Cable Chain
        Designer: Communication Arts Inc.

9458   Potato Patch Club
        Designer: Communication Arts Inc.

9459   Medical Couriers
        Designer: Communication Arts Inc.

9460   Healthworks
        Designer: Communication Arts Inc.

9461   My Friends
        Designer: Communication Arts Inc.

9462   Hiroshi Kira
        Designer: Communication Arts Inc.

9463   Southwest
        Designer: Communication Arts Inc.

9464   Colorado Federal
        Designer: Communication Arts Inc.

Index of Marks

Designers

5 Penguins, Design; 269 W. Alameda Ave., Burbank, CA 91052

Adam, Filippo & Moran Inc.; Design Consultants, 1206 Fifth Ave., Pittsburgh, PA 15219

Adams, James M.; Adams Graphic Design Group, 106 S. McKinney, Richardson, TX 75081

Advance Design Center; 4020 Oak Lawn Ave., Dallas, TX 75219

Bass, Melanie; 1358 N. Cliff Valley Way N.E., Apt. D-5, Atlanta, GA 30319

Beer, Henry; Communication Arts Incorporated, 1112 Pearl St., Boulder, CO 80302

Biles, William L.; Biles Design, 2990 Richmond, Suite 105, Houston, TX 77098

Brumfield, Debbie; D. Brumfield Design, 1314 W. Main St., Nacogdoches, TX 75961

Bullock, David & Nora; Graphic Design/ Illustration, 617 Luella Dr., Kutztown, PA 19530

Cats' Pajamas; 344 Ramsey, Saint Paul, MN 55102

Cheltenham, Eugene; 2224 Silver Ridge Ave., No. 4, Los Angeles, CA 90039

Chu, H.L., & Company Ltd; 39 W. 29 St., New York, NY 10001

Cohen, Emil M.; 2607 Kenilworth Ave., Wilmette, IL 60091

ComUnigraph Incorporated; 530 S. Grand West, Springfield, IL 62704

Connelly, Don; Don Donnelly & Associates, PO Box 536, 31 Avondale Plaza, Avondale Estates, GA 30002

Constance Kovar Graphic Design, Inc.; The General Design Store, 300 Woodbury Rd., Woodbury, NY 11797

Dellinger, Harvey; 39 McDaniel Ct., Greenville, SC 29605

Design Company, The; 12201 W. Burleigh, Milwaukee, WI 53222

Designed to Print, Inc,; 270 W. 73 St., New York, NY 10023

Dixon & Parcels Associates Inc.; 521 Fifth Ave., New York, NY 10017

Doremus & Company; Advertising/Public Relations, 850 N. Church St., Rockford, IL 61103

Engen, Scott; 9058 Greenhills Dr., Sandy, UT 84092

Engle, Ray, & Associates; 626 S. Kenmore, Los Angeles, CA 90005

English Finish Advertising Company Limited, The; 427 Woodlawn Ave., Cambridge, OH 43725

Farber; 385 S. End Ave., New York, NY 10280

Faye, Michael, Associates; 500 S. Sepulveda, Suite 304, Manhattan Beach, CA 90266

Ferraro, Armando S.; 3101-D Colonial Way, Atlanta, GA 30341

Fialkowski, Conrad; Suite 3260, 401 N. Michigan, Chicago, IL 60611

Fillhardt, Linda; Graphic Design, 236 N. Santa Cruz Ave., Suite 225A, Los Gatos, CA 95030

Follis Design; 2124 Venice Blvd., Los Angeles, CA 90006-5299

Forbes, F. Everett; 5913 Woodstock Ct., Virginia Beach, VA 23464

Frick, Paul, Graphic Design; 378 7th St., N.E., Atlanta, GA 30308

Gambetta-Bollmer Graphic Design; 5370 Leaf Back Dr., West Chester, OH 45069

Giarnella Design; 43 Linwood St., New Britain, CT 06052

Graphic Concepts; 4340 Carter Creek Pkwy., Suite 104, Bryan, TX 77801

Graphic & Photo Art; 2650 Mock Orange Dr., Salt Lake City, UT 84119

Harland, John H., Company; PO Box 105250, Atlanta, GA 30348

Heiman, Richard, Advertising, Inc; Tower Place, Penthouse Suite 2950, 3340 Peachtree Road, N.E., Atlanta, GA 30326

Hellman Design Associates, Inc.; PO Box 627, Waterloo, IA 50704

Hill and Knowlton, Inc.; One Illinois Center, 111 E. Wacker Dr., Suite 1700, Chicago, IL 60601

Horwitz, Mann & Bukvic Advertising; 2241 Losantiville Rd., Cincinnati, OH 45237

Hucknall, Nanette; 336-C Adolphus Ave., Cliffside Park, NJ 07010

Ikkanda, Richard, Design Associates; Graphic Design/Advertising, 2800 Twenty-Eighth St., Suite 152, Santa Monica, CA 90405

Image Network, Inc.; 645 West End Ave., 2B, New York, NY 10025

Keating & Associates; Advertising & Public Relations, 2223B Magazine St., New Orleans, LA 70130

Kelly, P.; 3415 Wyandot, Denver, CO 80211

Kinser, Bill, Design; Rd. 1, Boalsburg, PA 16827

Kosterman, Wayne, Associates, Inc.; Suite G, 955 N. Plum Grove Rd., Schaumburg, IL 60195-4757

Kramer, Miller, Lomden, Glassman; Graphic Design, 1528 Waverly St., Philadelphia, PA 19146

Kutchey, Valerie, Design; 702 N. Eutaw St., Baltimore, MD 21201

Landis, John K., Graphic Design; 438 W. Walnut St., Kutztown, PA 19530

Larrabee Design Associates; 940 N. Negley Ave., Pittsburgh, PA 15206

Lead Advertising and Design; 161 E. Chicago St., Elgin, IL 60120

Leigh, David; 1245 Park Ave., New York, NY 10128

Leitstein, Alan, Graphics; 8360 N.W. 21 Ct., Sunrise, FL 33322

Lesniewicz/Navarre; 222 N. Eric St., Toledo, OH 43624

Lienhart, James, Design; 155 N. Harbor Dr., Chicago, IL 60601

Longo, Stephen, & Associates; Graphic & Package Design, Suite 2C Colfax Manor, Roselle Park, NJ 07204

Lun, Andy; Graphic Designer, 270 Clinton Ave., Brooklyn, NY 11205

Lyons, Richard E.; Richard Heiman Advertising, Inc., Tower Place, Penthouse Suite 2950, 3340 Peachtree Road, N.E., Atlanta, GA 30326

Malone Group, The; 1420 Atlantic Bank Tower, Jacksonville, FL 32202

Matteson, Ron R.; 1638 N. Camelia, Tempe, AZ 85281

Mazzama, Maria; 255 Riverwoods Ln., Burnsville, MN 55337

McDonald, Max, Design Office; 5812 Alcove Ave., N. Hollywood, CA 91607

Mielcarek, Vincent J.; 106 Hatfield Place, PO Box R, Staten Island, NY 10302

Nervig, Carole, Graphic Design; 2120 Thirteenth St., Boulder, CO 80302

Neumeier Design Team; 212 High St., Suite 4, Palo Alto, CA 94301

Olson, Patricia; Cats' Pajamas, 344 Ramsey, Saint Paul, MN 55102

Palazzo Design; 1105½ Beach Ave., Bradley Beach, NJ 07720

Parker, David; Graphic Designer, 34-29 97th St., New York, NY 11368

Pavey, Jerry, Design; 14513 Melinda Ln., Rockville, MD 20853

Persechini & Moss; 357 S. Robertson Blvd., Beverly Hills, CA 90211

Pierce, Ron W.; (address unavailable)

PR Associates, Inc.; Advertising & Public Relations, 1799 Akron-Peninsula Rd., Akron, OH 44313

P.R. Design; 5971 Hillrose Dr., San Jose, CA 95123

Probst, Alison & Robert; 106 Hosea Ave., Cincinnati, OH 45220

Pullara, Paul, Graphic Design; 26 Meadow Dr., Little Falls, NJ 07424

Purdue University; Creative Arts No. 1 Bldg., W. Lafayette, IN 47907

Qually & Company, Inc.; Advertising/ Design/Firm, 2238 Central St., Evanston, IL 60201

Rabe, Peter J.; Graphic & Photo Art, 2650 Mock Orange Dr., Salt Lake City, UT 84119

Ramsden, Rosalie, Graphic Design; 7418 Burning Tree Dr., Houston, TX 77036

Runyan, Robert Miles, & Associates; 200 E. Culver Blvd., Playa de Rey, CA 90293

Schenker, Probst & Barensfeld; 2728 Vine St., Cincinnati, OH 45219

Settleducati, Mark; 218 E. 17th St., New York, NY 10003

Sharan, Jerry, Graphics; 44 Berkshire Rd., Sandy Hook, CT 06482

Shore Design; 250 Columbus Ave., Suite 203, San Francisco, CA 94133

Sloman, Gaynelle W.; Advertising & Design, 405 Capitol St., Suite 700, Charleston, WV 25301

Sommese, Lanny, Design; 481 Glenn Rd., State College, PA 16801

Tscherny, George, Inc.; 238 E. 72 St., New York, NY 10021

Vorisek, R. Seth; 151 Garden Ave., Paramus, NJ 07652

WW3/Papagalos Incorporated; 313 E. Thomas Rd., Suite 208, Phoenix, AZ 85012

Weller Institute, The; 2427 Park Oak Dr., Los Angeles, CA 90068

White, Carl; Doremus & Company, 850 N. Church St., Rockford, IL 61103

Yasumura/CYB; 100 Park Ave., New York, NY 10017

Young & Martin, Inc.; Graphic Communications, 550 Pharr Rd., N.E., Suite 835, Atlanta, GA 30305

Zahor Design Inc.; 150 E. 35th St., New York, NY 10016

Zarwell, Bob; The Design Company, 12201 W. Burleigh, Milwaukee, WI 53222